# Three Easy Magic Tricks

Sally Cowan

Photographs by Lindsay Edwards

**Three Easy Magic Tricks**

Text: Sally Cowan
Publishers: Tania Mazzeo and Eliza Webb
Series consultant: Amanda Sutera
  Hands on Heads Consulting
Editor: Sarah Layton
Project editor: Annabel Smith
Designer: Leigh Ashforth
Project designer: Danielle Maccarone
Permissions researcher: Corrina Gilbert
Production controller: Renee Tome

**Acknowledgements**
All photographs by Lindsay Edwards Photography © Cengage Learning
Australia Pty Limited, except those listed below.

We would like to thank the following for permission to reproduce
copyright material:

Front cover, pp. 5, 7–11, 17, 21–23 (background): iStock.com/ sommersby;
back cover, pp. 3, 4, 6, 12, 17, 18, 22, 23, 24 (magician vector images):
Shutterstock.com/NotionPic.

Every effort has been made to trace and acknowledge copyright.
However, if any infringement has occurred, the publishers tender their
apologies and invite the copyright holders to contact them.

NovaStar

Text © 2024 Cengage Learning Australia Pty Limited

ISBN 978 0 17 033393 1

**Cengage Learning Australia**
Level 5, 80 Dorcas Street
Southbank VIC 3006 Australia
Phone: 1300 790 853
Email: aust.nelsonprimary@cengage.com

For learning solutions, visit **cengage.com.au**

Printed in China by 1010 Printing International Ltd
1 2 3 4 5 6 7 28 27 26 25 24

*Nelson acknowledges the Traditional Owners and Custodians
of the lands of all First Nations Peoples. We pay respect
to Elders past and present, and extend that respect to
all First Nations Peoples today.*

# Contents

# Amaze Your Family and Friends!

Are you ready to amaze your family and friends with three entertaining magic tricks? Well, you have come to the right place!

A magician's job is to make people believe that something that seems impossible to do is possible. The success of the trick depends on the skill of the magician – that's you!

Magicians don't want their audience to know how they do their tricks. Make sure you keep your **props** and magic **methods** a secret.

Now, let's get on with the tricks!

**Magician's Tips**

* Practise the tricks many times before you perform them.

* Remain calm and confident in front of your audience.

* If you make a mistake, don't worry! Just wave your cape to distract the audience and start again!

For your magic show, wear some colourful clothes and a cape.

Keep your props in a magic box out of sight of your audience.

Use a small table with a plain dark cloth.

# A Clever Card Trick

## ✳ Goal

To tell your audience which card a **volunteer** has picked from a **pack** of cards – without you seeing it, of course!

## ✳ Materials

You will need:

☆ a pack of 52 playing cards with the two jokers removed.

**pack of cards**

**jokers**

# Steps

## Preparing the trick before the show

1. Divide the pack of cards into red cards and black cards.

2. Place the red cards on the top half of the pack.

## Performing the trick

1. Tell the audience, "For my first trick, I need a volunteer to pick a card!"

2. Hold the pack of cards with the patterned side up. Spread the cards out flat, like a fan, but be a bit sneaky: only spread out the top half of the pack.

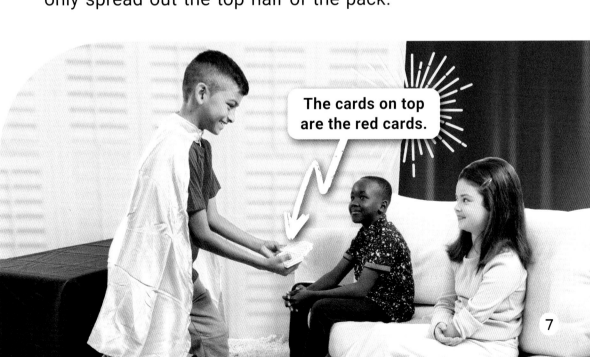

The cards on top are the red cards.

**3** As the volunteer picks a card, say, "Don't show me the card!"

**Magician's Tip**

Your volunteer won't realise that they are picking a card from just one half of the pack.

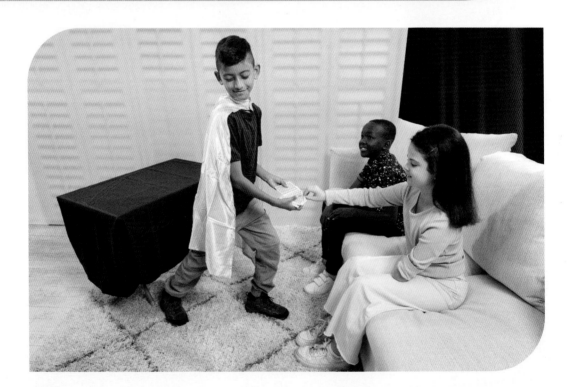

**4** Close the fan quickly and hold the pack in your hand, with the patterned side up.

**5** Tell your volunteer, "Remember your card and show it to the rest of the audience!"

**6** While the volunteer is showing the card to the rest of the audience, spread out the bottom half of the pack of cards.

The cards on the bottom are the black cards.

**7** Ask the volunteer to place their card back into the pack while you look away. Then, close the fan again.

**8** Tell the audience, "I will now say which card my volunteer picked!"

**9** Look through the cards as you hold them up with the patterned side facing the audience. You will see which card the volunteer picked, because the red card will stand out from the **surrounding** black cards.

It's easy to see the red card.

**10** Say, "I believe it was … the Queen of Hearts!"

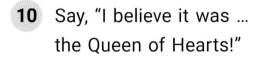

# A Brilliant Ball Trick

## ✳ Goal

To make your audience believe that three balls can magically jump through solid cups!

## ✳ Materials

You will need:

☆ 3 paper cups
of the same size

☆ 4 small pom-pom balls
of the same colour.

### Magician's Tip

Impossible? No! This trick has some fast hand work and a secret fourth ball that the audience won't see. *Shh*, never give away a magician's secret!

paper cups

pom-pom balls

# Steps

## Preparing the trick before the show

1  Place the secret fourth ball in a cup – this will be the "middle cup" during the trick.

2  Stack one cup on top of the middle cup and the other underneath it.

3  Place the remaining three balls in the top cup.

# Performing the trick

**1** Tell the audience, "For my next trick, I will make three balls magically jump through some cups!"

**2** Pick up the stacked cups and tip the three balls out onto the table. Put the balls in a row.

**3** Place a cup upside down behind each ball, starting on your left side. Carefully **rotate** the cups towards your body as you put them on the table.

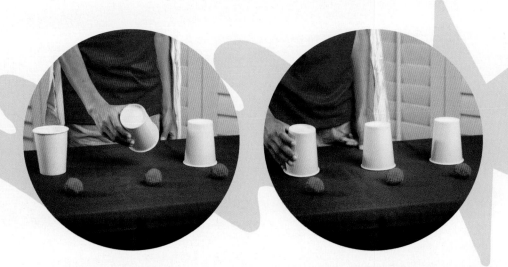

**4** Place the middle ball on top of the middle cup and stack the left and right cups on it.

**5** Click your fingers and say the magic words "Hey presto!" as you pick up the stack of cups. The secret ball will magically appear on the table, as if it has gone straight through the cup!

It's really the secret fourth ball!

**Magician's Tips**

\* Hold the cups low over the table when you rotate them.

\* Turn them in a **swift,** flowing movement so the audience won't see the secret fourth ball that's hiding inside the middle cup.

**6** Place each cup upside down on the table again in the following order: put the left cup behind the left ball; quickly cover the middle ball with the middle cup that has the secret ball in it; put the right cup behind the right ball.

**7** Place the left ball on top of the middle cup and stack the other cups over it.

**8** Click your fingers, then pick up the cups to show there are now *two* balls underneath.

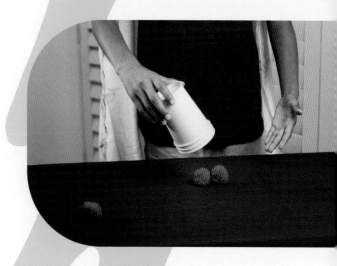

**9** Repeat step 6, but this time, cover the two middle balls with the middle cup.

**10** Place the right ball on top of the middle cup, stack the other cups over it and click your fingers! Pick up the stacked cups to show all *three* balls underneath!

There'll be excited gasps from the audience!

# A Crafty Coin Trick

## ✳ Goal

To make your audience believe that you can make three coins magically disappear

## ✳ Materials

You will need:

☆ 2 paper bowls with a wide **rim**

☆ 6 coins

☆ some double-sided **adhesive** tape.

Impressive? Yes!
This trick involves some sticky craft work.

paper bowls

coins

adhesive tape

# Steps

## Preparing the trick before the show

1   Cut three small 1-centimetre pieces of tape and stick them to one side of three coins.

2   Stick the three coins **firmly** inside one of the bowls. Make sure the audience can't see the tape!

3   Put the other three coins into the same bowl.

# Performing the trick

1.  Place the bowl with the coins and the empty bowl side-by-side on the table.

2.  Hold out the bowl with the coins in it, tipping it slightly towards the audience.

    Say, "For my final trick, I will make three coins disappear!" Point to the coins as you count them, "1, 2, 3, 4, 5, 6!"

    Jiggle the bowl to show that the coins are moving. Make sure no one notices that three of the coins are staying still.

3.  Place the second bowl on top of the first bowl so that the rims touch. This leaves a hollow space inside the two bowls.

**4** **Clasp** the bowls together tightly and turn them over three times. Make sure to count each turn out loud, "1 ... 2 ... 3!"

**5** Say some magic words: "Ta da!", or carefully remove one hand and click your fingers! Slide the top bowl off smoothly and place it upside down on the table.

Don't let the audience see the coins taped inside this bowl!

**6** Show the audience the bowl with the three loose coins left in it.

Take in the loud gasps from the audience!

When your magic show is over, take a bow!

Place all your props into the magic box. That way, no one will see how your tricks are done. Wave your shiny cape on your way out!

**Magician's Tip**

Remember to practise, practise, practise!

# Glossary

| | |
|---|---|
| **adhesive** (*adjective*) | sticky, like glue or tape |
| **clasp** (*verb*) | to hold or grip something with your hands |
| **firmly** (*adverb*) | pressing hard |
| **methods** (*noun*) | the ways that something is done |
| **pack** (*noun*) | a complete set of 52 playing cards, also known as a deck |
| **props** (*noun*) | items that are used to perform magic tricks |
| **rim** (*noun*) | the top outer edge |
| **rotate** (*verb*) | to turn, usually in a round action |
| **surrounding** (*adjective*) | on all sides of something |
| **swift** (*adjective*) | quite quick, but not too quick |
| **volunteer** (*noun*) | a person who does something without being told to |

# Index